I0012512

Alive in Social Media
How Digital Liveness is Redefining Our Identities

Challenges and Perspectives
after 25 Years of New Digital Uses

Laurent FRANÇOIS

Originally published in France under the title *Réseaux Sociaux : une communauté de vie*. © L'Harmattan, 2023, www.harmattan.fr

Daddy, does it really exist?

To Zachary, Ellie, Thien.

PREFACE

This essay was written between 2018 and 2022. A long time in the digital age, marked by unprecedented upheavals, including strict lockdowns.

For young French people, these lockdowns were likely their first experience of freedom deprivation.

While I thought these bewildering times would lead to a return to reality, to a kind of zest for life — and living — in the "tangible" world (clubs, bars, travel...), I also feel an acceleration of our hybridization as humans: a new reality lived, intertwined with digital worlds, made up of experiences without truly distinct boundaries.

A smartphone always in hand, a notification on the mind, a message to send. As if this liveliness — the notion we will attempt to define in the following pages — was deeply embedded in our neurons.

I do not know if this life, crossed — and sometimes conditioned — by social networks, is good or bad.

What I do know, however, when my son asks me if something really exists, is that it is increasingly difficult to answer unequivocally. First, because doubt seizes me on subjects that require long reflection to provide a simple answer; and also because parental authority on what used to be certainties can be contested with the opening of an app, a click.

Narrating lived experiences is no longer so obvious; other truths compete with each other, attempting to turn our attention into adherence.

The work ahead is unparalleled. For it will be necessary to establish a shared, positive societal vision while deeply understanding the mechanisms of social networks, the platforms that infiltrate our daily lives. In short, the search for the "first blood" in this battle, as in a video game, where the first hit or injury influences the rest of the adventure or game.

And to question what now seems innate: like those three little dots that appear in messaging apps when we are writing a text or sharing content, giving this bittersweet impression of life at our fingertips. At the reach of a touch screen. Three little dots – an ellipsis – born from a few lines of code, the brilliant intuitions of developers, coders, who like alchemists have transformed algorithms into an impression of life. Into liveliness.

FIRST BLOOD

"Real love is when you can't exist without someone, when you'd rather die than be apart, and the whole world goes dark, and nothing else matters but the person standing in front of you." *Euphoria*, Rue, S1.Ep3: *Made You Look*

THE LIFE OF OTHERS, THE LIFE OF ONESELF

In September 2021, French newspaper Le Figaro offered an analysis of the way young people in France speak. Among the expressions chosen was the famous "*ma vie,*" (*my life* in English) which signifies deep friendship between people, as in "*t'es ma vie*" (*you are my life*). This expression has exploded in conversations, translating to its use in instant messaging, hashtags on social networks, and everyday language.

Journalist Maguelonne De Gestas analyzed the success of "*ma vie,*" highlighting the importance of the feeling of presence brought by social networks: "*Does the phrase 'bring to life' not mean: 'animate someone, reassure someone, give reasons to hope, to live'?*"[1]

"*Ma vie,*" a powerful possessive adjective and common noun, marks belonging, connivance, possession, sensitivity, and the physicality of friendship. It's no wonder then that when a friend wishes a happy birthday to their comrade, they often do so through Instagram Stories, featuring them alone or together. It's a mark of affection, a mark of possession, where the friend will be notified that they are mentioned.

---

[1] https://www.lefigaro.fr/langue-francaise/expressions-francaises/petit-guide-de-traduction-du-langage-adolescent-a-l-usage-des-parents-20210917

"*Ma vie*" takes shape and reveals its feelings via social networks. As if, without being connected, friendship would have less flavor.

A LIFE MADE OF EVIDENCE, OF DIGITAL TRACES

To love, to live, one would need to exist online.

When we first open a social network, several questions are asked; of course, basic information: name, first name, sometimes date of birth. And very quickly, the network tries to understand our interests better, to see if other acquaintances are already members. Civil status is relegated to the background by what really interests the network: our billions of data and interconnections, our most implicit, complex wishes and aspirations. In other words: scenarios about our future states. Scenarios about what will make us want to spend time behind a screen, interacting with others, known or unknown. To feel their presence. Sometimes even to fall in love, to feel a sense of lack.

This change of state can be illustrated by the type of statuses — that is, those little messages or content posted by users — requested by different platforms.

In 2006, Twitter (now called X) posed for the first time a simple question that the user had to answer in less than 140 characters: "*What are you doing?*" Twitter was then in its early days and looked much like what we could find in chat rooms; after all, with only a few million users, Twitter was still a relatively niche place, populated by pioneers (bloggers, "internet people," journalists...). Nearly twenty years later, and with more than 300 million active users, the network of politicians, music fans, TV show enthusiasts, conspiracy theorists, and activists has significantly evolved its little prompter and now asks us all "*What is happening?!*" when we open the app. A concrete manifestation of our transition from a rather naive era, where the promise was initially to have fun chatting online, to a time when social networks and their ramifications not only witness the real lives of people but sometimes even supplement or replace them.

As if the statuses or publications that platforms constantly urge us to share were demonstrations, proofs of our existences, our feelings.

FROM BEING ALIVE TO BEING IN "LIVENESS": THE IMPACT OF SOCIAL NETWORKS

This is the thesis of this essay: social networks are transitioning humans from merely being alive to being in "digital liveness," that we can define as the quality or state of being alive.

"Liveness" is both a new form of life (connected, permanently), a substance (flows stemming from the use of social networks and feeding them), a state (feeling in "digital liveness" when we are active on a social network), and even a capital (transmitting a level of "digital liveness" to one's surroundings or even to one's children). It plays with the spatial and temporal dimensions created by the development of communication infrastructures like the internet. "Liveness" can be a great power: the more "digital liveness" an individual has, the more they can impose it on others. Conversely, those less endowed with "digital liveness" may begin to feel powerless, rejected, excluded, even hateful.

It questions humans' relationship to life: "digital liveness" can last beyond an individual's will, and even be transmitted peer-to-peer or through lineage. "Liveness" is created, found, lived.

"Liveness," created by the use of social networks, becomes as important to a growing number of individuals as air or water: it is through it that they feel alive or suffer, define themselves, love or hate themselves.

"Liveness" is measured according to a certain level of intensity, creating new criteria for evaluating our own lives, successes, or failures, impacting not only our relationships with others but also the kind of future we can envisage together. We will attempt to define this "digital liveness" in the following pages with the usual precautions: it is a living study object, influenced by both individuals and platforms, traversed by societal and economic changes; just as defining being alive, framing being in "digital liveness" can only be done by creating structures of understanding, to better grasp it... to better understand the stakes.

The purpose of this essay is not to be an introduction to the use of social networks or their future cousins like "metaverse." It is also not an attempt to list all possible user practices. However, we will use them throughout the pages to better track "digital liveness."

"Liveness" is studied by philosophers, media theorists, sociologists. It is also used by communication strategists, marketers, creatives who have well understood its power to influence people's behavior. We will draw inspiration from their work.

LIVENESS IS HERE

Four concrete manifestations of digital liveness allow us to better grasp its essence, if not fully understand it.

IN CRISIS SITUATIONS, THE VITAL ROLE OF ACCESS TO SOCIAL NETWORKS

First, one of the first things that associations provide to refugees is internet access, a fundamental tool for survival, following the recommendations of the United Nations High Commissioner for Refugees[2]: "Reliable mobile and Internet connectivity is critical to ensuring that refugees are able to access the economic and social benefits brought by the digital revolution, and to building broader connections between refugees and the communities and societies hosting them, as well as in their own countries. Through these connections, refugees are better protected, are able to become agents of their own development and that of the communities hosting them, and have the prospect of dignity and self-reliance."

For these millions of people, staying alive also means staying in digital liveness, connected to others to increase their chances of survival, and dreaming of building a better future.

We must quickly dispel clichés about this: for them, the smartphone is not a pastime but primarily a safety tool[3], a compass, to avoid being deceived by smugglers, to confirm routes, and check the measures in force at borders. It is also a genuine pocket navigator, connecting to the social fabric

---

[2] https://www.unhcr.org/innovation/internet-mobile-connectivity-refugees-leaving-no-one-behind/#:~:text=Refugees%20are%2050%25%20less%20likely,also%20a%20barrier%20for%20many.

[3] https://theconversation.com/le-telephone-portable-instrument-de-survie-pour-les-refugies-59945

whenever the smartphone finds a connection point. It's a way to stay in touch with family and also to carry out administrative tasks. In short, to be reachable and in digital liveness.

Numerous anecdotes in French television reports show Ukrainians and their host families placing the smartphone on the table and using Google Translate to understand each other. A way to integrate while learning the language continues.

Beyond refugees or migrants, all studies over the past 10 years prove that the internet is becoming as essential a resource as air or water[4]. And this, regardless of age, social background, or gender. The internet is in our lives, and it is a part of life.

DIGITAL INFLUENCE, NEW CAPITAL, POWER-LIVENESS

The second concrete manifestation can be found with influencers.

In 2022, the term *influencer*, which was once used to designate a person who objectively had the ability to impact others' decisions, now denotes a self-declared profession. A shift that is not only semantic but coincides with an evolution in our relationships with influential people.

To simplify, in the pre-internet era, influence could be measured along an axis of credibility/visibility; the doctor was — still — an unquestionable figure, and popular singers were launched by radio programmers, not by TikTok.

Then the first social networks equated the voice of a friend with that of a journalist or expert, in private bubbles

---

[4] https://newsroom.cisco.com/c/r/newsroom/en/us/a/y2011/m09/air-food-water-internet-cisco-study-reveals-just-how-important-internet-and-networks-have-become-as-fundamental-resources-in-daily-life.html

(the Facebook wall remains a prominent place for spreading messages against legitimate culture).

In 2007, Le Monde Interactif launched a new pure player, LePost.fr[5], at the height of citizen journalism and the first "buzz," while still maintaining an element of legitimacy through the authors' biographies and selection by a professional editorial team. It was truly in the United States and Europe that a turning point occurred with Instagram, allowing celebrities and their teams to gradually take over users' private bubbles. The Kardashians are the most obvious example of taking power over our social networks on a large scale.

This "social media" aristocracy also unfolds in less massive forms through niche subjects where leaders are over-represented by the platforms once they reach a certain notoriety. For literature lovers and those who enjoy beautiful love stories in French, the Amours Solitaires[6] account on Instagram, launched by Morgane Ortin, found a brilliant niche: documenting people's romantic exchanges by sharing screenshots of their texts or other private messages. This account is now almost always suggested to a new social network user. As if these accounts were devouring all the tiny spaces of attention, and thus people's private space. Moreover, already popular accounts are pushed to a vast number of users rather than favoring emerging content creators, which tends to amplify their power.

This aristocracy imposes its digital liveness on our attention span, around which our "real" friends must now coexist. Unlike television, where a celebrity can disappear or be skipped, there are few examples of personalities losing all their followers in record time, even after scandals

---

[5] https://www.clubic.com/actualite-301468-benoit-raphael-lepost-fr-rester-inventif.html#message
[6] https://www.instagram.com/amours_solitaires/

or bad buzz; as if crime could go unpunished on social networks.

Social media aristocrats also try to prepare the next generation, as if to better transmit this digital liveness capital; famous families like the Beckhams have all gradually launched their sons or daughters with support for their digital presences, often around a main interest (an art, a cause, etc.). Brooklyn Beckham is a good example; the Beckhams have strongly supported this aspiring photographer in his vocation.

Far from a simple favor as old as the world, we have witnessed a true story factory: legitimizing the son's talent, progressively spreading seemingly candid shots, a game of hyper-personal documentation to create belief for buying.

In this case, the Beckhams wanted to give digital liveness to Brooklyn's desire before pushing his photographic work. A storytelling that nevertheless led him to photograph a campaign for Burberry, representing decades of work for accomplished photographers if they are not named Beckham. Liveness is profitable.

The family has also been accused of nepotism. Irony of history, since Brooklyn Beckham has since changed his focus, now dedicating himself to the role of a chef, and his Instagram account no longer gives much space to photography. A flaw his detractors often point out: creating digital liveness, if the story is ultimately just a bad copy of advertising, generates disapproval and disaffection of communities — but not their disengagement: Brooklyn Beckham's 14.4 million Instagram followers are still there. A real inheritance, partly inherited, and to be capitalized on.

This aristocracy is now attacked by platforms like TikTok, which replace the follower/following logics of historical networks like Instagram (I still need to follow an account on Instagram in 2022 to regularly see its content) with discovery logics where technology imposes the digital liveness I will be exposed to.

On TikTok, there is no need to follow or subscribe to an account: the algorithm decides the type of content that will be served to me, based on millions of criteria, soon billions of individuals.

Instead of categorizing content traditionally (e.g., cooking, fashion, cats, etc.), TikTok invents its own categories, its own "sides," through a concatenation process that illuminates how the network operates: basically "a group of things linked together or occurring together in a way that produces a particular result or effect"[7]. In some programming languages, it means chaining two lists or two strings of characters end to end or even a juxtaposition and chaining of linguistic units in a given order.

In other words, TikTok constantly analyzes sequences of emerging actions, then suggests them to users resembling those who initiated these sequences. TikTok assumes a margin of error in this system and adjusts in real-time the criteria and audiences to serve these increasingly precise contents. Human creativity being limitless, users find themselves working for the network by providing these logical sequences; content creators, in turn, detect an opportunity and create content for these new logical sequences.

Examples abound: just in the last three weeks of December 2022, we saw an explosion of beauty tutorials replicating the impression of crying with makeup (#cryingmakeup), and a surge of clips of rappers reciting texts by great writers and philosophers. TikTok wants to "glue" us to these sides to maximize time spent on its platform, creating a kind of zombie digital liveness, perched on a type of content consumption that makes it hard to detach from the smartphone.

---

[7] https://www.merriam-webster.com/dictionary/concatenation

DISAPPEARING FROM SOCIAL NETWORKS, VIOLENCE AGAINST THE OTHER

Another concrete manifestation lies in a new expression that has entered worldwide conversations: being ghosted.

Ghosting is a way of breaking contact without any explanation. Overnight, the person stops giving any sign of life.

This rupture of contact, felt violently by the victim of ghosting, is certainly not new; but as we are permanently connected, not giving any sign of life to messaging contacts is perceived as the ultimate punishment, even as something rude.

Jacques Derrida enlightens us on this subject: "The proper of a specter, if there is any, is that one does not know if it testifies by returning from a past living or a future living, for the revenant can already mark the return of the specter of a promised living. Untimeliness again, and misalignment of the contemporary."[8]

Ghosting is in itself a misalignment of digital liveness. The analogy with the figure of the ghost is also interesting: the only sure thing is that the ghost testifies to something that was and could have been, probably the absurd demonstration that created digital liveness, when it disappears, leaves an empty space.

LIFE BEYOND THE SCREEN: THE ROLE OF EMOJIS AND STICKERS

The last example of concrete manifestation: the explosion of emojis and stickers, these small static or

---

[8] Jacques Derrida, Spectres de Marx, Paris, 1993, Galilée, p. 162, quoted by Lionel Ruffel, « Le temps des spectres », in Bruno Blanckeman and Jean-Christophe Millois (éds.), Le roman français aujourd'hui : transformations, perceptions, mythologies, Paris, 2004, Prétexte, pp. 108-109.

animated drawings that are part of our daily exchanges. These were born out of the need in conversations to add emotions but also from a constraint: the length of texts users could send via SMS.

Designers like Shigetaka Kurita had to create 176 emojis as early as 1999 for a new mobile internet service i-mode, where the brief was to find graphic shortcuts to express both ideas and interactions, with the constraint that a user could only use 250 characters per message. It's no coincidence that this achievement was first realized in Japan, due to ideograms and advanced digital usage, with populations seemingly more capable of using new emotional signals to reduce conversational frictions. In short, to charge their interactions with digital liveness.

This technology/emotion playground has become sophisticated, with most social networks integrating the ability to add "reactions" to posts (as on Facebook).

The graphic or creative choice of the network has significant consequences: in the case of BeReal, the network strongly encourages users to record reactions themselves with their smartphone camera, which can then be automatically published under the followed people's content. Emojis and their evolutions allow complementing what words sometimes struggle to express in instant messaging exchanges; they allow the user's emotions to break through the screen and deeply impact the interlocutor.

An incarnation-emotion concentrated in small graphic objects, which somehow come to life physically in the memory of a smartphone and the user's language habits. They are, in short, condensed emotions, desires, life overflowing through a technological intermediary, which inversely transforms the physical world, everyday life; as if a buffer zone, a new space overflowing both into people's minds and their lives, is being created.

This is, of course, true from a cultural point of view with the passage of codes or signs born from these conversations into everyday life (the emoji is used to measure people's satisfaction both in shops and now in hospitals!). It is also true from a societal point of view: no need to be Arthur Rimbaud to master the codes of good conversation: everyone, regardless of their level of education or culture, can suddenly appropriate these tools and "perform" with them.

"You know, computers aren't the thing, they're the thing that gets you to the thing". Halt and Catch Fire

PHYSICALITY IN THE DIGITAL WORLD, THE BODY OF LIVENESS

Liveness is a long learning process. We often start quite awkwardly on a social network or in a virtual world, as if we suddenly become clumsy and unskilled. For older individuals at the dawn of widely accessible internet, it was first necessary to physically struggle to learn how to type on a keyboard, to move a mouse cursor. Some people still type with just one finger on the keyboard.

PHYSICAL TRAINING FOR DIGITAL USAGE THAT GIVES BODY TO LIVENESS

A rather violent training, with its share of frustrations but also satisfactions once the device is mastered. For younger individuals, intuitive navigation through the touchscreen begins even before reading, deeply embedding the use of hands — and thus the body — in digital environments. Many criticize the impact of screens on the brain, but we must also focus on the inscription of these physical gestures in the flesh of young humans.

THE VERB OF LIVENESS: FINDING ONE'S TONE TO CREATE ONE'S DIGITAL BODY

Once the basic uses are better understood, a first tentative message is sent, a form of greeting to the planet. An action, often attempted on a whim, is launched, without necessarily having read all the rules or having gone through all the tutorials. For the more daring, on the other hand, the first act in a game or on a social network takes on the somewhat vain appearance of having found one's tone, rules, and style... In short, the ambition to formalize from the start the expression of one's personality and the reading contract offered to one's future audience.

Initially, it was only text on the first social networks, but video gradually took over, with the TikTok phenomenon and new networks like BeReal, whose concept is to post one photo per day at a specific moment imposed by the app, using both the front and rear cameras of the smartphone. This further enhances the impression of authenticity or chosen moments, in a less figurative way than text but with a raw, physical, unfiltered side. A window into our lives, in digital liveness.

In this ocean of possibilities, there is the desire of everyone to bring their small voice and find their little (or big) space; as Lynn Hcrschman Leeson reminded us, "the idea often determines the medium."[9]

Where digital liveness takes root in our lives, it is because it does not remain solely in the realm of ideas but also in the physical world. Liveness needed to be born.

---

[9] Surface, issue 150, Guerilla Girls

WHERE DOES LIVENESS SPRING FROM?

Let's start with where digital liveness draws its life: language, correspondence, and its need for a response from the other. A language reshaped, accelerated, geographically and temporally extended by the power of instant messaging, social networks, and all the technological functionalities of apps.

A NEW SPACE CREATED BY LANGUAGE IN THE DIGITAL

This reshaped language passes through dense, complex infrastructures, machines with phenomenal computing power, through pipes and cables that we often tend to forget. It is interesting to note that one of the basic notions between a device (smartphone, computer) and a server is latency; the ping allows us to see the time it takes for a small packet of information to travel to the server and back. Specialists can then determine if the connection is lagging (or in jargon, lag). This measure is somewhat akin to measuring the intensity of digital liveness; if it seems too diffuse or lengthy, it is perceived as potentially problematic by people.

These messages are not just a substitute for real-life conversation. They open new territories of thoughts, ideas. Instant messengers are increasingly augmented. Filters, long perceived as anecdotal by novices (we've all played with cat or dog ears appearing while calling a friend on video), are one of the revolutions that mix traditional conversation with the game of language, and increasingly a certain level of physicality. Instagram, for example, through its augmented reality software Spark AR, quickly introduced the ability to create effects based on hand gestures or body movements.

Sending a kiss can be visually concretized during a video call; automatically translating sign language as well, modifying the context around us can now be done with a body movement... the examples are endless and accessible to the general public. Apple Vision Pro is now supposed to bring a new era of spatial computing.

ENRICHED LIFE, AUGMENTED DAILY LIFE

This digital liveness springs from these conversations and social networks that gradually open new ways to express it, to give it body. By launching features sparingly, iteration after iteration, we enter a beta conversation, to use developer terminology: social networks expand, test our capacities to adopt and learn new uses, to intensify our exchanges. In a way, every time a social network introduces a new feature, it acts as if submitting it to a more or less consensual referendum to users. If users adopt it, this feature will become an essential component of the platform. Conversely, it will lead to its removal, a modernized version of the thumbs-down (in Latin *police verso*) of ancient Rome.

A recent example is the Project Convey launched in the United States by Cox with the creative agency 180LA. Conversing through video calls can be a major problem for many people on the autism spectrum, who may have difficulty reading the emotions and expressions of their interlocutors. Using facial and auditory recognition technologies, the system developed by Cox helps users better read their interlocutors' emotions with emojis. And thus join this form of digital liveness, more inclusively[10].

The strength of digital liveness is not only in its role in the intellectual world: it has penetrated popular culture, everyday culture, of (almost) all people. Impossible to imagine in some cultures the absence of the little daily message. Family, friends' WhatsApp groups are part of a very real daily life. We pass by, consult the chats — or the silences, by the way — return, activate or deactivate notifications.

FROM A SUBSTITUTE CONVERSATION TO A NEW SOCIAL ORGANIZATION OF RELATIONSHIPS

Perhaps at the beginning of the internet, digital liveness was a substitute for a rational problem: a cousin living in another country, a long-distance love, an exchange between university researchers at a distance. There was a need to go to a network or messaging to reduce the distance between people.

Today, digital liveness is much more than a substitute for the physical being: it accompanies our identities, our relationships, our lives. It allows us to check in or convey attention. Liveness draws its... life from simple needs or deep desires. Dating platforms give pride of place to chatting, for better or worse. Buying on Craiglist or Vinted also involves a messaging system. Who hasn't found themselves excitedly waiting for an auction confirmation on eBay? Or getting annoyed with their phone against an unscrupulous user on Blablacar? In this sense, the distinction between "real life" and "digital life" is an intellectual shortcut, a vain ready-made thought: there is

---

[10] https://newsroom.cox.com/2022-04-06-Project-Convey-by-Cox-Provides-Meaningful-Connection-via-Video-Conferencing-for-Individuals-on-the-Autism-Spectrum

only one life, increasingly intensely traversed by digital liveness.

Liveness certainly accompanies our new connected selves, and it is also thanks to the strength of designers, developers, and engineers that it has developed, driven by the developments of digital platforms and their ever-growing appetite for new users... and making them stay. Meta — formerly Facebook — measures its effectiveness through an explicitly named indicator: Teen Time Spent[11]; and to achieve this, one of the engines seems to be digital liveness: becoming a place where the user returns almost mechanically, where they can worry if a message is not read by a friend, a space that becomes almost physical where we show ourselves, hide, miss each other. Live. No wonder Meta — like other businesses — believes so strongly in the promise of the metaverse: a new stage in the human-machine interface.

This digital liveness already has many repercussions on the construction of our identities, our emotions, on the role of platforms, and raises ethical questions.

---

[11] https://www.nytimes.com/2021/10/16/technology/instagram-teens.html

A NEW ORGANIZATION OF DIGITAL LIVES NOT WITHOUT AMBIGUITY AND RISKS

Where there is the origin of digital liveness, there is also the authenticity of this digital liveness. Developments in artificial intelligence and graphic rendering allow the creation of fake characters, either based on real people — the famous deepfakes — or pure creations. This is not in the interest of social networks: Facebook, through its FAIR (Facebook Artificial Intelligence Research) lab, tried as early as 2019 to invent an artificial intelligence that could counter the exploitation of user videos by facial recognition software by applying a filter. The network fundamentally needs real users; if they start to believe too much in deepfakes, the transfer of digital liveness to fictions could break the value chain of networks like Facebook. There is a fragile balance between the digital liveness of real user to real user and all the technological means that give body to this digital liveness, excite it, prolong it.

Liveness needs humans to exist, while humans continually invent features and technologies that give it new modes of existence, new incarnations. If there is fluidity, it is in the hybridization of desires enabled by technology for humans: it not only gives them the possibility to realize their fantasies but to give them digital liveness, thus becoming real for those who want to believe in them.

Liveness also exploits the fear of loneliness. In the United States, 36% of Americans report feeling severe loneliness[12], and this percentage increases among young adults and women with young children. Feeling like waiting for a response or sensing a presence is a form of substitute drug; it's no wonder that French intellectual Michaël Stora

---

[12] https://mcc.gse.harvard.edu/reports/loneliness-in-america

spoke as early as 2017 about "digital comfort objects" (or in French *doudous*) regarding smartphones.

Liveness is transmitted and concretized peer-to-peer; it is important to look back to better understand the genesis of digital liveness. The digital world also has its history; let's go back for a moment, about 20 years, an eternity on the internet scale.

IT WAS ALL ABOUT EMOTIONS AND MESSAGES IN BOTTLES

"And I can't see you here, wonderin' where am I
It sort of feels like I'm runnin' out of time
I haven't found all I was hopin' to find"
Arctic Monkeys[13]

Social networks have been both a major actor and a consequence of what is commonly called Web 2.0 since 2004; without delving too much into technical considerations, Web 2.0 allowed the separation of the container (a web page model, a blog model, a Facebook profile model, etc.) from the content (a text, an image, a video). Before Web 2.0, publishing an article required significant technical knowledge, programming skills. In short, it was a territory reserved for professionals and coders.

Thanks to the work of millions of developers, this more participatory web gave birth to tools where internet users, even without technical background, could open a blog, publish content, and share it. A fact we take for granted in 2022, which was a fundamental pillar of digital liveness. In 2003, the blogging platform WordPress, for example, was launched, offering millions of individuals the possibility to blog for free.

WEFEELFINE, THE FIRST PROJECT TO VISIBLY CONCRETIZE LIVENESS

In March 2006, the microblogging platform Twitter was born. And in 2006, a significant project was born:

---

[13] Arctic Monkeys (Alex Turner) paroles de *Why'd You Only Call Me When You're High?* © Emi Music Publishing Ltd

Wefeelfine.org, which absorbed all online conversations starting with the phrases "I feel" and "I am feeling," from blogging platforms like LiveJournal, MSN Spaces, MySpace, Blogger, Flickr, or Google.[14] Through the continuous scrolling of unknown internet users' quotes, researchers discovered one of the levers of social networks' success; not just finding a solution to a problem or a way to share a passion, but all the elements that invite their users to return, independently of an immediate need: the feeling of belonging, the sensation of being heard, the occupation of the mind through the occupation of others.

This project, viewed from 2022, may seem naive, as philosophical quotes on Instagram, live confessions on TikTok, or public stances on Twitter are now commonplace.

A LIVING SYSTEM, PEER TO PEER

Twenty-five years ago, Wefeelfine was the first attempt to visualize digital liveness; by aggregating RSS feeds — a technology whose "main advantage (...) is to easily follow an information flow (for example, new articles on a news website) without needing to manually visit it using a web browser[15]," the platform allowed us to understand all human heartbeats, all emotions, already shared online.

The platform, by absorbing all feeds from major social networks (which were much more open at the time) and blogs, allowed for the first time to see a sort of map of our emotions, a planetary-scale (at least anglophone) ultrasound of humans in digital liveness.

The creators referred to it as an almanac to prove that social networks follow certain seasonality and that the traces left on them are influenced by context, mood,

---

[14] https://number27.org/wefeelfine
[15] https://en.wikipedia.org/wiki/RSS

environment, etc. Thus, Wefeelfine allowed for comparisons based on the day's weather and to prove its impact on our online conversations. The project concretized what early users of social networks and, more broadly, Web 2.0 began to feel: we are connected by our digital words and part of a larger whole. We follow logics that are anything but binary, giving body to something that takes us with it.

THE WISDOM AND MADNESS OF CROWDS

Wefeelfine.org grouped all these exchanges into madness, whispers, montages, crowds, mounds, and measures, creating groupings around emotions at will. A partial view of online exchanges but one that illuminates our digital liveness and its complexity more than twenty years later. The montages allowed for creating collages, inspiration boards around an emotion; the whispers gave the impression, line after line, of an endless dive into our deepest feelings. The crowds offered the possibility to filter based on socio-demographic criteria and easily see similarities, connected links. An organized chaos, ultimately, mixing formats and expression media, depending on what users do with social networks.

The proof that a user opens a profile not to make it a destination but as a living, moving entry point, a pivot for their connections and desires.

What was really new was seeing how people who did not know each other could share similar traits, whether joys or anxieties, or any other feeling, desire, passion, virtue, or vice. These groupings — artistic and scientific in the case of Wefeelfine — also anticipated the foundations of advertising in social networks: segmenting user groups based on extremely fine criteria, far beyond obvious criteria like age or gender, to then suggest ads to user groups similar in their uses and desires to the first analyzed group (the famous "lookalike audiences" for advertisers). The Cambridge Analytica scandal highlighted years later the scandalous abuses of this type of targeting[16]. Ultimately, it was people's digital liveness expressed through data in their

---

[16] https://www.theguardian.com/news/2018/mar/17/cambridge-analytica-facebook-influence-us-election

most intimate aspects that was sold for political purposes, without ever being consented to.

A LIVENESS THAT PENETRATES ALL BORDERS AND BODIES

2006 thus justified millions of individuals who began to express themselves online: "I" was no longer alone, as somewhere, someone could be moved by a tiny digital trace left in any way, accessible by anyone who knows how to search.

Social mechanics emerged on discussion forums or in blog comments, often to the creators' surprise.

On Doctissimo, users' concerns quickly transformed into almost friendly relationships. Users began to check in on each other, exchanging quickly via private messages. It's no wonder that Doctissimo quickly grouped "maternity" discussion threads based on the month of term: by observing their communities, the platform quickly realized that beyond the questions asked, users (mainly women) returned to encourage each other; grouping them by term allowed small groups of women to share a very addictive experience.

The blog of Yoani Sánchez in 2007 is a textbook case[17]; to circumvent censorship in Cuba, she mobilized her community to amplify Cuban voices, passing texts through a network of friends via USB sticks to publish her daily life outside Cuba; digital liveness already far exceeded the internet's scope, with the creation of real social networks.

Human communities began to gather on the internet, anonymously or not, around a common interest. In fact, Web 2.0, the technological tool, allowed for the development of real living communities, with rights and

---

[17] https://www.nytimes.com/2011/07/06/books/yoani-sanchez-cubas-voice-of-a-blogging-generation.html

duties, mutual projects, solidarity phenomena (or exclusion), without necessarily meeting physically.

The username sometimes became an individual's primary identity on certain social spaces; and for community members meeting for the first time at a physical event, the username was the natural way to call or address each other.

These logics are now found on almost all social networks or messaging platforms: Telegram loops where actions are organized are the spearhead of political activists[18]. But it is also where parents discuss classroom life.

This also helps digital liveness take such a strong hold in our lives: it infiltrates social networks whose objects are very broad, versatile: on the same tool, a terrorist can recruit a future martyr while a grandmother can organize her next outing with her grandchildren. The supposed neutrality of the platform is never complete: the chosen features structure the type of interactions that ensue. It is certainly not guilty, but it has a part of responsibility for the actions that interlocutors want to undertake. Even acting as a catalyst in extreme cases: it is because a first terrorist broadcast a first attack live that other individuals could be inspired by it. Liveness as scattered as life, in short.

Human contacts established from the beginning of social and media networks created this habit, this reflex; if social media allowed people to express themselves in front of others — consciously or not, through simple publication technology, it was its democratization that made these links so important and then so lively; what was almost an unintended consequence became the raison d'être of social networks, whatever the subject or interest.

Probably the continuation of the beginnings observed in the United States on IRC chat systems (which sometimes

---

[18] https://www.lemonde.fr/pixels/article/2022/04/22/telegram-base-arriere-et-opaque-du-militantisme-en-ligne_6123307_4408996.html

grouped several tens of thousands of users simultaneously), or in France on voila.fr or Caramail chats.

With a decisive moment being the arrival of unlimited internet access, pushing people not to have to go to a discussion space but to stay there permanently.

In France, Free was the first to launch an unlimited internet plan in 2002 for less than 30 euros, which effectively set a standard and exploded usage.

A DEFINITION CHARGED WITH ISSUES: MONEY AND POWER AT THE HEART OF THE NETWORKS

From the origins of the term social media in American English, two major currents seem to emerge:

- An American approach, which understands the term media in the sense of a communication or advertising channel. From the outset, therefore, the transactional relationship seems to be embedded.

- A more European approach, which emphasizes the social aspect, thus opposing the advertising dimension of social media.

This tension at the very genesis of social media is still present more than a decade later; especially among those who want to benefit from social media by transforming this digital liveness into money. Brands, of course, but also politicians.

LIVENESS, A TOOL FOR CONQUEST AND MAINTAINING POWER

In the case of Donald Trump's election, a philosophical question arises: to what extent can one use the social media channel to achieve one's own ends, even if it means implanting a fiction that completely replaces reality?

By revisiting the credibility/radiance axis, the platform fully played the post-truth card: to a complex reality, bring a simple narrative (a good story and especially an intrigue), create heroes and give roles to the actors of this narrative, and of course, make the audience itself become actors.

The audience becomes actors to varying degrees. This can be through simple involvement in a vote or supporting partisan content; specifically, making sure a topic emerges on the Reddit platform by upvoting a particular thread is a way to express interest... and play a role. Through the repetition of these actions, individuals develop habits, a social fabric; and question less the why of these actions because their role becomes evident, alive. The audience can also become responsible for the success of an initiative, not only by performing tasks within an organization's framework but by defining roadmaps, steps, projects where they must imagine mechanisms, think about recruiting, acquiring new members, in short, imagine a true scenario leading to an economy of digital liveness.

This fabricated and repeated story replaces a certain degree of truth, probably due to the adherence processes instituted throughout its creation, and the impact it has on the daily social life of people who adhere to it. On the other hand, the truth has perhaps deserted these new mechanisms of persuasion or at least has not known how to use them as skillfully. Post-truth takes life — and digital liveness — through social networks and then the social life of a large part of Americans as a whole.

LIVENESS IS RESILIENT

As difficult as it is to create digital liveness — this force that attracts users who move within it and becomes a center of gravity — making it completely disappear is a most complicated task.

Unplugging the connection by suspending certain controversial social media accounts does not cut off the digital liveness their authors have managed to create. Donald Trump being banned from Twitter on January 8, 2021, did not prevent him from continuing to shine and enjoy his digital liveness with his community. The mechanisms of digital liveness, when misused, are quite similar to those activated by certain religious cults. The goal is always in the end to make believe — thus to replace what was considered normal or obvious with a new set of values or social fabric; and to "make do," that is, for the convinced to in turn preach, thus recruiting new followers to ensure the system's survival.

There are no more limits to the absurd when the generated adherence is sincere: Thomas Pesquet, usually very measured in his statements, had to explain again in 2022 that humans did indeed walk on the moon, speaking strongly on social networks and in the media[19].

Nonetheless, it is no longer just a few eccentrics fueling conspiracy theories, but millions of users spreading their own truths, which eventually take digital liveness.

In Donald Trump's case, the transactional dimension became almost religious, like a modernized version of a quest asked of believers. Among the myriad of tools used by his supporters, direct contact, emailing, is a mass evangelization weapon. It's not surprising that the alt-right social network Gab ends each of its newsletters with "parallel economy" where businesses with similar values should pay for ads like a quest: "We can't do this without you. We ask for your prayers. (...) Finally we ask that you prayerfully consider supporting us by upgrading to GabPRO, purchasing some merchandise from our shop, or running ads on Gab for your business to reach an audience of people who share your values (...). To God Be The Glory, Andrew Torba CEO, Gab.com Jesus Christ is King of Kings."

Sacha Baron-Cohen's indictment of Mark Zuckerberg eloquently illustrates how those who master the use of social networks or media can, in a way, steer the object of digital liveness for their own ends: "on the internet, everything seems equally legitimate. Breitbart looks like

---

[19] https://www.lexpress.fr/actualite/sciences/thomas-pesquet-et-le-complot-lunaire-pour-les-scientifiques-la-fake-news-de-trop_2179442.html

the BBC. The rants of a lunatic seem as credible as the findings of a Nobel Prize winner. It seems we have lost a shared sense of basic facts on which democracy depends."

Similarly, when a platform like Meta decides to change the rules of the game, especially by modifying its algorithms or design, it creates winners and losers. On July 23, 2022, photographer @illumitati launched a petition against Instagram to "return to Instagram" (in other words, to revalue photos rather than videos to align with TikTok). 48 hours later, Kylie Jenner and then Kim Kardashian shared this petition on their social networks, generating thousands of articles and forcing Instagram to seemingly backtrack. A logical reaction and stance considering how much their businesses depend on their Instagram accounts; Kim Kardashian's grid and color choices can even influence millions of people in their purchasing decisions!

THE TECHNOLOGICAL ORGANIZATION OF SOCIAL NETWORKS HAS IMPACTS ON POWER

The truth is that Meta did not decide to change Instagram and backtrack because of the Kardashians and petitions: it's because Meta's business is being shaken by new rivals like TikTok that Meta is trying to glue users to the future without alienating the existing base. A difficult balance to find, proving that platforms like Meta always risk disappearing or dying.

Another essay would probably be needed to address digital liveness in China; nevertheless, through super-applications like WeChat (which allow chatting with friends, ordering food, paying, meeting friends...), the regime has managed to apply the concept of social harmony to a sort of giant intranet on its territory; mixing social, transactional, cultural, and social destinies within a single ecosystem. Liveness is thus even stronger, not by multiplying tools but by forcing a kind of unique playground with unmatched functionalities in the world. The dream of many social networks or platforms: to control concatenation in a closed environment. This allows valuing all the user's history on a platform and better dominating future uses: past data meeting future data, in short.

The influence of the technological organization of platforms on users also explains why dominant networks apply copy strategies (not to say plagiarism) of new features exploding among new actors. Faced with the success of BeReal — the famous dual camera system we discussed earlier — TikTok, Instagram, or Snapchat decided to introduce the same type of feature within weeks. This is to prevent potential user migration to new networks. Liveness is an explosive substance.

Its definition is political, and its potential creates control desires. Digital influence strategies develop, creating new markets with fierce competition to capture people's available attention and try to frame their next actions.

In the United States, young athletes' contracts stipulate increasingly precise rules on their social networks to maximize profits, while player associations like the NBPA attempt to quantify the value of young players' digital presence. Liveness is a long-term investment.

Is digital liveness similar to word-of-mouth marketing? In other words, radiance allows substituting for credibility safeguards, with digital liveness becoming a stronger form of truth in all sectors, giving reason to Edward Bernays over a century ago: "those who manipulate this unseen mechanism of society constitute an invisible government which is the true ruling power of our country.[20]"

Perhaps an overly simplistic view of digital liveness, but one that explains at least partly the current mistrust against

---

[20] Propaganda, Edward Bernays (trad. Oristelle Bonis), éd. Zones, 2007 (ISBN 978-2-35522-001-2), p. 31

both the holders of legitimate power, new influencers, and social networks.

In a 2021 Gallup report conducted in 21 countries for UNICEF's Changing Childhood Project, while 15-24-year-olds use social networks for information, only 17% of them trust them a lot; while only 61% trust health professionals (doctors, nurses, etc.) a lot[21]. This tends to prove that digital liveness is a boon for manipulators of all stripes while also adding to the era's confusion.

LIVENESS, A SOURCE OF INEQUALITY AND DISCRIMINATION

Should this digital liveness be deserved or earned?

It is a real challenge that institutions, or even brands, are just beginning to address; after building communities or connecting to them, some now have millions of followers, with varying degrees of participation. As a real media, the question is now how to give back some of the digital liveness to certain followers, to favor them, highlight a talent or desire. Every time a brand creates an Instagram story highlighting an artist, it certainly gives them some notoriety but above all, it makes them a subject of discussion, a subject of digital liveness to a broad audience.

The question remains whether major actors and users of social networks will seriously identify the potentials within their followers — and thus contribute to a certain vision of the world, notably by providing tools to those with ideas but not necessarily all the assets to succeed — or remain in convenience. It's relatively easy to relay someone already known or who has a certain level of notoriety, someone who has already done all the work, than to set up real engineering at the community's service. During the Black

---

[21] https://news.gallup.com/opinion/gallup/357446/young-people-rely-social-media-don-trust.aspx

Lives Matter explosion, we saw that mechanisms could be established to promote businesses or projects bringing change. But how many organizations continue to use their digital liveness in this direction, beyond the reaction they may have provoked? Meritocracy and short-term priorities — especially the annually renewed or not marketing budget — do not always go hand in hand, including in digital liveness.

ATTEMPTS TO REGULATE AND ORGANIZE LIVENESS ARE STILL INEFFECTIVE: GROWING DISCONTENT

New community models, such as communities attached to servers on Discord, offer more virtuous prospects. A user generally must adhere to a charter with rights and duties. There is moderation work carried out by both the organization and super-users, hyperactively. Groups usually also have a roughly clear roadmap on the purpose of the Discord server. These servers fully play the digital liveness card: first, because structurally, one of the columns always on the screen shows active users, giving this impression of life; and because they rely on the ability to generate relevant conversation, always encouraging contributors to express themselves.

Not having comments under a post on Instagram is not dramatic, but a Discord server essentially requires strong conversations.

It remains to be seen if decentralized models can become the norm, or if they will remain the preserve of highly involved communities, highly targeted around an ultra-specific project, but limited in total user numbers.

Pushing the reflection, the subject of social scoring of individuals as happening in China, or to a lesser extent the logics of verified accounts on social networks, is a ticking time bomb, with digital liveness at its heart. Algorithmically, classifying users is not new. Databases aim to segment and theoretically make services more efficient. However, at a societal level, we risk letting platforms, networks, partially dictate at least what deserves other users' interest, what should be primarily followed and suggested.

If the phenomenon was already problematic on television, it could still be humanly and politically addressed. In the United States, there are between 1500 and 2000 TV channels depending on the year, very few compared to the billions of users frequenting social networks, where networks decide who has more digital liveness. Scoring, in its most advanced form, can be a tool for controlling a population, clearly assumed by Beijing; but it also has more insidious drifts in other regions: the little blue badges on Instagram are a way to officialize that one account is more important than another.

But the criteria remain extremely opaque: some record companies have privileges, immediately giving one of their protégés this famous certification; but isn't the university professor not connected to the decision-makers and yet influences — or simply teaches thousands of people — more important? The subject of overweighting one individual over another is explosive: just read the criticisms against Elon Musk during his attempt to launch paid authentication on Twitter without verification[22].

Once again, digital liveness has variable geometry forms and expressions. The certainty for me is that the subject is far too serious for public authorities to leave it solely to the market; its form does not necessarily have to be measured on a success scale with winners and losers but to be

---

[22] https://www.liberation.fr/economie/economie-numerique/reseaux-sociaux-elon-musk-sous-le-feu-des-critiques-apres-le-lancement-chaotique-de-la-certification-twitter-bleu-20221114_VR3VPACSCBG65B26CEIP6DZZXY/

apprehended through new criteria, the societal vision being at the heart of the reflection. Liveness can be one of the greatest opportunities for humanity to exist better, together. It requires engineering, a vision from all actors, not just to benefit from its media dimension — reaching people — but also to nourish its social dimension — creating links.

A pious wish for now if we look at the statistics: in France, 70% of students are in a state of discomfort according to a study for the LMDE mutual insurance[23]; the main actors of digital liveness, hyperconnected, the first generations not to have known a world without the internet, are prey to discomfort that connectivity has not resolved.

And we could cite hundreds of serious studies worldwide confirming this youth discomfort, for whom social networks are one of the problems, and too rarely solution providers. Stories of cyberbullying occupy the space, as do those of indoctrination or self-confidence destruction. Liveness shapes us, and we shape it. Nevertheless, digital liveness is created through technological platforms, which mediate, alter, or sublimate our desires and connections. Every platform has a bias, but digital liveness has a definite impact on our futures.

A real battlefield whose consequences on marketing or communication we barely measure, but on our lives and relationship to... the living.

---

[23] https://www.francetvinfo.fr/sante/psycho-bien-etre/sante-mentale/70-des-etudiants-sont-en-situation-de-mal-etre-selon-une-enquete_5248942.html

HISTORICAL SOCIAL FACTS CROSSED BY SOCIAL NETWORKS

Let's try to take some obvious examples of the impact of social media, of digital liveness, on our daily lives, especially in social phenomena known to all: marriage and suicide.

MARRIAGE: THE IMPORTANCE OF DIGITAL FOOTPRINT

Lacoste, July 4, 2018; a traditional Provençal wedding; thirty-somethings dressed to the nines, a jazz band accompanying the wedding party to the bride's childhood home; rosé wine and smiles.

There are a few differences from a Pagnol novel: the songs are recorded and shared almost live on Instagram; friends have maintained their connection since their student years thanks to Facebook; the caterer was found online after consulting numerous reviews; the film edited by the newlyweds themselves in an improvised cinema in the woods is composed of clips recovered from YouTube.

In the small assembly present, cousins and siblings were of course part of the celebration; and among them were "internet friends": a modern term to describe people we exchange with — sometimes daily — on Instagram, Messenger, or whom we met long ago on enthusiast forums.

French marriage law itself is interesting and disrupted by digital liveness.

"Marriage is both a republican institution and a solemn contract, a public and legal act. The two people who marry commit to each other, before and towards society, to respect the rights and duties governing this institution. In return, they ask society to recognize the existence and value of their mutual commitment and to ensure the protection of the law.[24]"

The "before and towards society" aspect now has an increasingly important digital dimension where the social environment and the way the environment testifies to the marriage are socially validated and traversed by social networks.

Before society: the testimony of the union tends to be increasingly documented via social networks. This documentation can be encouraged by the networks themselves, which see it as a way to qualify the lives of their users, thus federating or engaging them. In extreme practices, it can even become dangerous, as in the case of sextapes! Facebook introduced relationship status options (open relationship, married, in a relationship, etc.) to keep the networks of lovers up to date. LinkedIn's addition of pronoun preferences (e.g., She/Her) in 2021 also clarified one's orientation before their network[25]. A practice intended to be more popular in the United States but ultimately impacting all regions of the world. Many applications play on this field. Google Photos allows increasingly refined content curation, not just chronological (memories from 1 year ago) but affinity-based (memories together, just the two of us), sent not only to the user but also to their social graph. This poses many problems: when to cut the circuit of digital liveness, especially in the case of a divorce, death, or separation? A growing issue that goes beyond the right to be forgotten: if individuals control part of the love story, it becomes relevant to be able to put an end to it quickly.

Towards society: this is undoubtedly the most complex area; however, legal — and moral — obligations are

---

[24] Fiche pratique sur le mariage, Ministère de la Justice
http://www.justice.gouv.fr/publication/fp_mariage_civil.pdf
[25] https://www.lemonde.fr/economie/article/2021/10/12/afficher-ses-pronoms-de-genre-se-banalise-dans-les-firmes-anglo-saxonnes_6098075_3234.html

increasingly traversed by social networks. Family life is more scrutinized than before; some lifestyle choices are publicly politicized, attracting or repelling certain users. A personal commitment is also publicized, consciously or not. The interaction induced by this documentation can validate an individual's role or invalidate or cancel it[26].

SUICIDE: FROM THE LAST LETTER TO LIVE STREAMING

The example of the suicide of Vietnamese artist Plaaastic (real name Mai Nhi) has become one of the most troubling known cases. A social media phenomenon, she became known through widely shared photographic and fashion performances on social networks.

Despite her evident success, content was posted on her Instagram account[27] (since deleted) and her Facebook page announcing her death.

This post generated thousands of comments as investigations were conducted by the artist's fans themselves. Numerous rumors spread, theories were discussed, plans hatched. So much so that in 2018, the artist reappeared in a long, striking video where she confessed that her suicide was fake[28]; she didn't provide specific answers but left her community with a cryptic message, explaining that she never sought to become a "viral idea" and that this video would only reach those who would search for her in the future.

A prescient message as she ended her life, this time for real, a few weeks later.

---

[26] https://www.radiofrance.fr/franceculture/podcasts/affaire-en-cours/cancel-culture-ce-n-est-pas-faire-table-rase-du-passe-c-est-precisement-l-inverse-1241236

[27] https://marcusleeyang.medium.com/plaaastic-lived-2ac141bc0c13

[28] https://archive.org/details/plaaastic-an-explanation

Although her book "Error 404" was never published in English, in 2020 fans of Plaaastic undertook the translation of the book on Wattpad[29]. A digital liveness that took precedence over the artist's life and also raises the question of controlling the narrative of our lives. Plaaastic's death paradoxically gave a new mission, a new life to a community of interests: to valorize her artistic legacy — which is not so new — but especially to recruit new members, new fans, giving digital liveness instead of life to Plaaastic.

This can be concerning because millions of Plaaastics now exist on social networks: can one control their own death? Last wills seem to be a thing of the past: if by accepting to be in digital liveness an individual grants a right to followers, then it is the followers who will have the final say online. The heritage legacy is also in full revolution: if Plaaastic "still exists," who will potentially receive royalties? Who will be most able to manage her posthumous reputation? Platforms attempt to set up tools like Meta's trusted contacts feature; however, an individual's reputation and digital liveness extend far beyond their profile on a single network, making the answer still quite weak.

The boundaries of the sacred are shattered, including in its most extreme deviations. How many religious fanatics have recorded a testimonial video before committing an attack? A behavior now obligatory for certain terrorist organizations, as if God not only waged war but also streamed the performances of his martyrs, regardless of their camp. A proof of the act that now seems attempted to be broadcast live, on Meta, Snapchat, or TikTok. As if existence could only be effective if reported by audiences, confirmed by a panoptic gaze. Observers believe it is for

---

[29] https://www.wattpad.com/779913180-error-404-plaaastic-english-translation-part-1

organizations to nurture their audiences and attract new targets; I think it is for those committing these actions to feel all-powerful, immortal, by forever freezing their digital liveness. In other words, an act, a situation (positive or negative!) can only truly exist if they enter digital liveness, meaning they leave a digital trace, a publication. In some subcultures like skateboarding, recording a video was the ultimate proof of an individual's talent, an undeniable proof.

It seems this logic of documentation, of testimony, is now the norm in every aspect of society.

Behaviors that have become common, because they have become daily, ordinary; yet hiding a staggering upheaval for our future humanities.

RADIO OR CASSETTE: PRECURSORS OF LIVENESS

To understand the notion of digital liveness, a detour to pre-internet media is enlightening.

In 1985, Joshua Meyrowitz established a difference between listening to a cassette in a car radio and listening to a radio station[30]. For Meyrowitz, listening to a cassette cuts the listener off from the outside world, while a radio station, even hyper-local, can always cover external information, whether national or international. In other words, the same content and the same flow can play a role, have a utility and a strong impact depending on the user's lived space. "Media change the social temperature[31]" according to Marshall McLuhan.

And the forms of digital liveness experienced by users change drastically depending on the social networks and interfaces deployed. Ultimately, what happens in the user's head is what matters, and the way content, signals are absorbed is as important as the signal itself.

LIVENESS REQUIRES USER ADHERENCE

The experience of content gives it a different life and has implications for the user that are unique to them. This is a key principle for understanding social networks, media, and even future metaverses: there is a principle of adhesion to create for digital liveness to take place.

All social networks, even before reaching a critical mass of users, seek to create a form of plebiscite with their first members. Like on the radio, Facebook's initial form was simple: are you ready to post something on your "wall"? On

---

30

http://eprints.lse.ac.uk/52423/1/Couldry_Liveness_reality_mediated_2004.pdf
[31] https://www.persee.fr/doc/colan_0336-1500_1969_num_2_1_3737

Twitter, the referendum could be summarized as: will you share what you are doing? On BeReal, the constraint is stronger: will you accept to post a diptych photo of what you are doing, at a fixed time? It is interesting to see that all new-generation social networks are much more precise — even dictatorial — than pioneering platforms: capturing a niche by combining more precise uses facilitates understanding the interest of registering for yet another network.

LIVENESS, LIFE BUBBLES IN A CLOSED CIRCUIT?

Another lesson from the radio and cassette example is that each network tries — explicitly or not — to favor forms of bubbles, with a life of their own inside them. Like a place a person enjoys (a garden or a café), the strength of a network is to generate returns independently of whether there is new content per se. I return to these places because I feel good there; because I know what to expect. Familiarity creates habit (and vice versa), digital liveness. These spaces of digital liveness remain fundamentally always open. In France, during August, it's not surprising that shopkeepers put "exceptional closure" signs on their storefronts when they go on vacation, as if to specify that the break in activity is almost accidental. The same goes for social networks: when a platform "falls," is no longer accessible for an indeterminate time, phenomena of excitement and irritation occur. When Instagram, Facebook, and WhatsApp were inaccessible in October 2021, millions of messages from users went to... other social networks. This proves that digital liveness may be born through a social network, but the connection created by users quickly transcends a single platform, overflows.

A meta-network that transcends the initial encounter... but paradoxically cannot live without social networks. It remains to be seen if the permanence criterion of relationships in major social networks will change the way digital liveness is organized, since at this stage, the historicity of profiles is relative: most platforms push a form of perpetual present (on TikTok, Snapchat, Twitter), while the granularity of relationships truly operates through private messaging attached to these social networks. Even Facebook, whose initial component was to be a sort of giant yearbook, has broken this logic.

There is a deep link between the type of digital liveness created and the form of the social network, functionalities, mode of operation. In the case of the Meta ecosystem, when the three main services fall simultaneously, it's a daily tool that is suddenly out of service. Like when a smartphone is down or forgotten at home: our social navigator is missing. A capacity to consume content but especially to exchange on the more private parts of the network. On Instagram, one of the most important factors was precisely this more personal part beyond the constant flow of beautiful images. People started exchanging, flirting, trying for a fling, or simply connecting, sharing their own discoveries, between two users or through larger groups. A fabric that exists parallel to the more public part of the social network, ultimately giving it its identity, its meaning.

LIVENESS, A GRADUAL ADHERENCE TO DEEPER AND DEEPER FUNCTIONALITIES

Before achieving such success and adoption of platforms, each social network generally offers a differentiating feature, a little something on which it will base its story.

Instagram managed the feat of being the fastest platform to upload and share a photo when loading times were still significant due to mobile offer limits. BeReal, as mentioned, imposes a game of double photography (selfie and what we see in front of us) without possible retouching, without the possibility of cheating by sharing a previously saved photo on the smartphone, with a time constraint and the obligation to share content to see others' photos. From this start, users will often begin to divert the original feature, develop modes of expression specific to the platform and communities that will gather and frequent it. It's almost impossible to know how digital liveness will metamorphose even if platforms can favor certain exchanges or directions; however, it is possible to anticipate certain behaviors based on previous social networks' experience. On the negative aspects, of course: setting up control systems against harassment by private message, avoiding trolling phenomena.

On the positive aspects, especially: encouraging virtuous behaviors on the network by giving rewards, unlocking access.

TEXTUAL COOPERATION
(Umberto Eco)

Umberto Eco developed many analytical frameworks that can help understand digital liveness and its emergence. Eco explains that there is a form of unconscious in the text; for a text (or content) to be accepted, enough readers (or users) must understand more or less the same thing; textual cooperation between the author and the reader involves countless codes, meanings, nuances, references; if in a book, the reader can only read, imagine, and then discuss, the shock is seismic on social networks: instant reaction, interactions, openness to the anonymous other.

A BATTLEFIELD OF SYMBOLS, INTERPRETATIONS, UNDERSTANDING

Textual cooperation takes on the appearance of a battlefield, which can also explain the violence that occurs online around ideas that come to life.

This is where digital liveness requires a certain framework for the user: when their content — for example, a tweet — is shared by hundreds of thousands of other users, their original intention may be misinterpreted. Their "normal" base of followers simply has superior reading keys, which can give them a shared language, implicit codes. Beyond the rules established by the social network itself, communities create habits and practices of their own; dynamic stage directions. Signs that are sometimes incomprehensible to outsiders, which can even lead to misunderstandings or misinterpretations. A debate not so new since punctuation itself was the subject of many discussions as early as the 19th century. "As early as 1841, Belgian lithographer Marcellin Jobard envisioned many new emotional punctuation marks, including points of irony, irritation, indignation, and hesitation, all represented by arrows pointing in different directions. His proposals, made to the Academy, however, remained dead letters.[32]"

The ability to generate the correct interpretation is an art online. The account of Etienne Dorsay[33], a brilliant interpretation of a fictional famous French actore (Jean Rochefort) led energetically by Gérald Arno, managed to generate this textual cooperation, while succeeding in lasting and sharing the existence of this fiction with millions of people.

COMMUNITY MANAGERS, THE G.O.s OF LIVENESS FOR BRANDS?

Less intellectual (although), the talent of community managers at Decathlon, Burger King, or Netflix France consistently hits the mark for communities for whom these accounts now hold significant importance in their daily lives. They replace the old radio stars: familiarity with the content, the impression of knowing them, the importance of small rituals, the creation of their own codes and insider secrets that bring life and spice behind our screens.

---

[32] https://www.radiofrance.fr/franceculture/une-histoire-de-la-ponctuation-point-d-ironie-et-point-de-doute-la-ponctuation-poetique-6537190
[33] https://www.nouvelobs.com/chroniques/20220102.OBS52775/un-hymne-a-la-banalite-les-meilleures-chroniques-de-la-photocopieuse-d-etienne-dorsay.html

BEYOND THE TEXT

This mechanism no longer relies solely on text; "hypertext" links had already accelerated the complexity of this cooperation by taking a user from one resource to another, from one medium to another. Navigating link by link requires voluntary action from the user. Links imply a form of two-dimensional experience, moving an individual from one point to another, like on a map.

A MORE PRESENT LIVENESS, THEREFORE MORE INVISIBLE IPSO FACTO

The strength of current networks (or virtual worlds) lies in the fact that these links are increasingly invisible in the user's experience.

Additional content is pushed by a subtle balance between the power of prescription and the power of suggestion; what once required typing a string of keywords into a search engine is now almost pre-established without the user taking any action other than browsing, exploring a platform. Liveness has an existence even in the most passive uses of networks.

THE TIKTOK MODEL

TikTok has already replaced Google for millions of individuals by replacing Google's injunction, search, with a new injunction, discover[34]. Links thus seem to transform into a quasi-magical substance, a bottomless well of content interesting to the user who dives into it. This quasi-physical dive is probably what captures the user's attention the most, pushing them into a state of flow well-known to

---

[34] https://fr.techtribune.net/google/passez-sur-google-tiktok-est-le-moteur-de-recherche-incontournable-de-la-generation-z-adweek/394613/

psychologists and the video game industry: "Flow (...) is a mental state reached by a person when they are fully immersed in an activity and find themselves in a state of maximal concentration, full engagement, and satisfaction in its accomplishment. (...) Flow is characterized by the total absorption of a person in their occupation.[35]"

Text, which involved a significant cultural or intellectual capital, has been replaced by other media that allow businesses to run their systems and reach critical mass faster. This can create massive inequalities between users who understand part of the networks' workings, possess legitimate culture, and those who suffer a double penalty: inability to understand usage and lack of access to legitimate culture. This does not mean that opportunities do not emerge precisely for users who could not have succeeded without these social networks.

---

[35] https://en.wikipedia.org/wiki/Flow_(psychology)

EXTIMACY AT THE SERVICE OF LIVENESS?

Social media superstar Lena Mahfouf summed up the new paradigm of celebrity in the social media era: "an actress gets into her characters' skin, me, it's my own skin[36]."
A shift between fiction, reality, presence, and fully assumed familiarity where the individual who tells their story seems traversed by thousands of other selves.

THE LIVENESS OF THE MOST KNOWN PERSONALITIES, A CAPITAL SHARED WITH THE PUBLIC

The difference from pre-internet celebrity can perhaps be analyzed in the impression of permanence, semblance of accessibility, and disintermediation between the celebrity and their fans, propelled by social networks. This can be double-edged: the artist Christine and the Queens, who has been presenting as male for several months, has been constantly attacked in the comments of her TikTok account[37]; criticisms of celebrities are not new, but the systemic and systematic nature is the consequence of this extimacy that makes people, voluntarily or not, public, publishable, publicized. Reachable.
Pascal Morand, regarding the marriage between Chiara Ferragni and Fedez, raises the question of the technological, business, and digital liveness[38]. "This fairy-tale universe

---

[36] https://www.nouvelobs.com/mode/20220801.OBS61572/lena-situations-une-actrice-se-met-dans-la-peau-de-ses-personnages-moi-c-est ma-peau-a-moi.html#modal-msg
[37] https://www.gqmagazine.fr/pop-culture/article/christine-and-the-queens-regle-ses-comptes-sur-tiktok-apres-des-critiques-sur-sa-consommation-de-cannabis
[38] https://www.lesechos.fr/2018/09/la-chronique-1020827

and 4.0 romanticism are less superficial than they seem. They reflect contemporary immaterialism, where the brand and creative spirit, entertainment, and games of imagination take precedence."

The notion of extimacy can help understand this playground. Without delving too deeply into Jacques Lacan's work, we can simplify its definition with a schema where, first, users tend to share information, their stories, anecdotes, most intimate feelings with a community of friends or strangers. Secondly, there is a magnifying effect in the opposite direction: the individual can live very intimately, very sensitively, events that are initially totally foreign to them, even in regions or cultures of the world with which they had no prior affinity. This is evident in exceptional situations like attacks or natural disasters; it is now the case for situations closer to our daily lives as well. Deborah James, better known as @bowelbabe on Instagram, launched a podcast on cancer; while she was now in palliative care, her last weeks were marked by immense support from millions of strangers; she even received the honorary title of Dame after approval from Queen Elizabeth II.

The reunion of twin sisters born in South Korea and adopted by two families 6000 km apart led to a documentary, Twinsters: it was through the discovery of a physical similarity in a YouTube video shared by a friend of Anaïs Bordier, one of the twins, that this quest for meaning began. Another example of the link between interconnections, communities, and digital liveness.

EXTIMACY, RECIPROCITY: THE QUESTION OF LIVENESS INFUSION

This extimacy of lived moments — or experiences — is in deep metamorphosis. While the web until 2020 allowed ultimately two-dimensional exchanges (hypertext links, photo and video sharing, etc.), the web in formation is opening a new dimension whose scope is still poorly understood. The third dimension, more sensory than textual, will very likely further intensify extimacy — and thus digital liveness — for humans: haptic technologies are already present in 2022, subtly on smartphones (the intensity of a vibration to touch, the impression triggered on certain notifications).

Inside a bubble, therefore, where the reciprocity of exchanges (or at least its impression), each other's desires, aspirations, social validation, represent some of the drivers of addiction to this digital liveness.

Some examples of reciprocity generated by this extimacy can be listed:

- Absolute recognition for a fan of an influencer is to be liked: that is, to receive a mark of attention from the admired person (note that the action is very often generated by bots or community manager teams…)

- The possibility of accessing more exclusive content: on Instagram, the close friends feature allows distributing brownie points by opening a part of oneself to a limited number of followers

- Social networks offer users tools to ask questions to their communities; the user can then choose which questions, which contributions to feature in a story; being chosen by the user, especially if they are known, is a form of accomplishment. We often see fans taking screenshots when they receive a like or a notification from their favorite influencers, who were curious enough to visit their account

- Super-fan badges based on a user's activity level give them a certain power; on Discord, which serves both as a chat server and forums, some users are rewarded with higher roles, similar to moderator or voice roles on chats 20 years ago. A free activity that rewards people who allocate significant time to the community, whether by providing precise insights (like on the case of Gucci Vault[39] who ran for a couple of years)

- Chatbots and other instant messaging management tools can give the impression of truncated digital liveness; however, when well-configured, they help better manage the incoming message flow, qualify them, and potentially respond more effectively and impactfully; proving that digital liveness always maintains this ambiguous relationship with the technological and transactional, real conversation and feigned conversation to achieve an objective.

Hyperlinks have in some way been partly replaced by hyperlinked individuals, in digital liveness.

---

[39] https://medium.com/@lilzeon/i-went-on-gucci-vaults-discord-server-this-is-what-i-ve-learnt-a3d41da41dd5

LIVENESS: THE ELEMENTS THAT GIVE THE SENSATIONS OF LIFE

For Ferdinand de Saussure at the end of the 19th century, language was comparable to a sheet of paper — thought is the recto and sound the verso — 150 years later, the new language operating on social networks, platforms, or other devices and platforms has given birth to digital liveness.

THE LINK BETWEEN DIGITAL IDENTITY AND LIVENESS THROUGH SOCIAL SCIENCES

Fanny Georges, a semiologist at the Université Sorbonne Nouvelle, is a pioneer in France of digital identity and self-representations on the internet[40]. In an interview for the Collège des Bernardins, Fanny Georges explains that there are three types of forces shaping digital identity[41].

1. Declared identity: what one declares about oneself on the internet, the image one wants to give of oneself, often flattering. Note that platforms force users to no longer only communicate static business card-type information (e.g., diplomas, careers, etc.), but increasingly dynamic (e.g., pushing the user to post stories, even on professional networks, encouraging more and more niche news).

2. Acting identity: the signs one leaves online, either by oneself or by the actions of others (e.g., if we are tagged in a post). This system is not only used on social networks but on all platform businesses, starting with Uber, Doctolib, or Deliveroo.

3. Calculated identity: a quantification of our identities (e.g., number of friends, likes). This calculation can be

---

[40] https://www.dailymotion.com/video/x5dkuqd
[41] https://vimeo.com/187143014

more or less sophisticated depending on the regions and users. Social scoring in China represents at this stage the highest level of tracking user data, at the cost of a certain renunciation of individual freedoms.

These forces around identity resonate with the flows pushed by social networks and digital platforms. The semiologist proposed one of the very first definitions of digital liveness in 2010[42]: "the term (…) designates the impression by which users feel the representation and the virtual world as part of their sensitive and lived experience. (...) The metaphor of flow introduces into the computerized structuring of the self information essential to the impression of life and movement of representation."

I believe this definition deserves to be pushed even further, 15 years later, in light of current and future uses: digital liveness is no longer just an impression; it has taken shape, it physically impacts, it can give meaning to life or lose people, it can determine future societal choices.

LIVENESS IS REAL LIFE, REAL LIFE IS LIVENESS

Liveness is not a separate playground from the real life of individuals: it is real life, in real life, it is the experienced, felt experience for the vast majority of users. Liveness is not just a representation of oneself, conscious or consensual: as we interface through technological means with other "selves," digital liveness certainly impacts how we act and narrate ourselves.

---

[42]

http://culture.numerique.free.fr/publications/ludo10/georges_ludovia2010.pdf

LIVENESS HAS BECOME AS NATURAL AS BREATHING

Liveness draws its strength from the fact that the individual does not think about it (or no longer thinks about it) when they live their life; digital liveness is both individual (my feeling, my life), mutual (what drives me to gather with others on a platform), technological (interfaces, technologies that give it shape).

Liveness exists even when the user is not consciously, actively interacting online: it is part of them, others are or will be part of it.

This acceleration of digital liveness follows technological and societal acceleration: if in the early days of the internet, the username allowed hiding, disguising behind an avatar — and thus preserving a semblance of anonymity — the main social networks quickly require official personal data: a phone number often linked to our real identities, but also increasingly frequently a copy of an ID. It is no longer just an impression of life in which my virtual "self" begins to have a manifest existence: it is my "self" that has a manifest existence, through digitized expressions either 100% (in some virtual worlds), or in a hybrid way (e.g., augmented experiences from the physical world, like playing with a Snapchat filter, conversational experiences on social networks). It remains to be seen in which spaces the user decides to express their digital liveness: choices are broad, ranging from Hikikomori in Japan, who have literally closed the doors of their rooms, to dancers who re-enchant urban areas like so many stages on TikTok.

THREE LITTLE DOTS:
The impression of life driven by social media and platforms' interfaces

The search for indicators of digital liveness in a digital environment can date back over twenty years, and it is at IBM that one can look[43]. Jerry Cuomo, an IBM Fellow and IBM's Vice President of Blockchain Technologies, created the first Typing Awareness Indicator. In a chat, when a user is typing something, other members are aware of the action being taken.

The experience continued, refined — initially, users could see in real-time what the other was typing — and reached its peak with Apple. Instead of showing a "text" indication, Apple proposed replacing it with the now-famous three little dots, still in use today on iMessage and adapted in various forms by nearly all instant messaging apps. Citing Fanny Georges, these three dots can be some "of the signs that carry within them the touch of the gesture that produced them."

INDICATORS OF LIVENESS, BETWEEN TECHNOLOGICAL WILL AND TRANSFORMATION BY USE

What started as a tool to communicate more functionally within teams of engineers or developers quickly turned into an expression tool, a social, romantic game, an artifact that can either generate anxiety or, on the contrary, open the

---

[43] https://www.sfgate.com/tech/article/typing-message-indicators-Jerry-Cuomo-IBM-text-15740983.php

floodgates of dopamine[44]. This seemingly simple tool has enormous consequences: the user "feels" what the other is doing, both physically and emotionally. By playing with the intensity of messages, the speed of response, aborted response attempts, and restarts, the tool creates tension between the stakeholders. Well-documented in pop culture, these three little dots have many cousins and multiple extensions, now subtly orchestrated by platform creators, social networks, or other metaverses. Each social platform has, more or less, attempted to organize the relationship with the other; what was initially about technical rules (when to send messages, in what format, who moderates, etc.) quickly turned into almost political rules, or at least rules that try to organize their communities. Tinder is a political system, just like Doctolib, Fortnite, with rights, duties, rules of the game, sanctions. A user who cheats or abuses a platform may be banned; they can always create a new account with a new phone number, but the systems are quite well made, and they will lose all their points, privileges. In a more virtuous system, the "good" elements of a social network are valued, with more rights, the ability to unlock levels, access. On Google Maps, local guides who contribute the most to the platform earn levels, giving them access to special offers. On Instagram, Twitter, getting a certified or verified account has the aura of a Grail, giving the impression of being more important than another user. Of having a superior digital liveness.

---

[44] https://www.nytimes.com/2014/08/31/fashion/texting-anxiety-caused-by-little-bubbles.html

PRESENCE INDICATORS
FOSTER LIVENESS

Discussions I can have in my work with artistic directors and user experience specialists often start around an obsession: how to capture and then maintain a user's attention? How to both satisfy their need and surprise them, capture their attention through many imperceptible signs.

We quickly realize that there is no generic solution — or only to be a copy-paste of existing models. This does not mean losing users in unintelligible codes or signs; rather, it means getting into more familiar details with a little twist.

IT'S ALL IN THE DETAILS

Small icons in the address bar of a web browser, animations when a page loads, are some tricks that allow for adding smart friction. Instead of just providing a solution to a problem, we try to bring digital liveness.

Many examples play with the tension between absence and presence. On MSN Messenger, which was one of the first tools to discover the power of instant messaging for many French people, a green icon signaled that a person was online when the internet everywhere, all the time, was still a luxury. A friend's connection launched a little jingle, while a new message had a different sound.

On WhatsApp, the seen today/yesterday mentions in conversations with users give an indication of when a friend or contact was active, or alive, on the platform: this little artifact can trigger various emotions, reactions. If the person hasn't replied to a message while they are active, irritations may arise. On the contrary, if the person seems to have been inactive for several days, worries may arise. No wonder that on social networks, if a person disappears too long for certain community members, then followers check to ensure everything is okay.

In its physical dimension, WeChat is one of the few mass platforms that integrated the "gesture" dimension from its inception. Shaking one's smartphone can suddenly connect a user with a stranger, thousands of kilometers away, adding a reified dimension beyond a simple swipe on an app like Tinder.

RECURRENCE AND REPETITION FEED LIVENESS

To exist online — and have greater digital liveness — most platforms, social networks, or metaverses invite us to act repetitively, routinely. The classic case is Facebook, which fully utilized its users' birthdays: a notification sent in the morning allowed everyone to wish the best for a friend. BeReal, as we have already mentioned, forces posting at specific times to give a stronger impression of authenticity. Instagram suggests posting stories from the past daily, a way to bring previously created content back to life, make it a new publication opportunity, and possibly trigger reactions from the user's followers.

VALUING THE MOST FAITHFUL ACTORS OF LIVENESS

In some virtual worlds, logging in several days in a row earns points, allowing access to tools, goodies, levels; on Amazon, repeating a purchase can save money; to grow one's community on most social networks, it is important to post frequently, publicly, at the risk of disappearing. On Google, leaving reviews on businesses or places visited increases credibility and thus access to better offers, beyond the pleasure of having a more substantial social badge. Some social networks or platforms have failed to maintain a strong enough value proposition for these recurring tasks to avoid becoming ultimately tedious. Foursquare, which perhaps best captured the check-in habit, signalling one's presence in a place to a user base, failed to take its community further: the social function was lost along the way.

This does not mean that every user desires digital liveness or wishes to conform to these platforms. However, it is cmerging that through social pressure, dependency, or structural choices, digital liveness becomes one of the capitals defining individuals.

NOTIFICATIONS: AN ARTIFICIAL AND PERSISTENT LIVENESS

Paradox of our connected individualities: we exist consciously and especially unconsciously beyond what we can control; and this because of notifications. Platforms, for the vast majority, need to reach a critical mass of users and ensure this mass returns constantly — including in current metaverse experiences — notifications remain at the heart of their business. And it turns out that notifications not only relay information that a friend or contact has just published but also amplify our behaviors to myriads of strangers. Instagram now pushes content from millions of unknowns amidst our truly chosen content; TikTok pushes us to discover — a euphemism for the word consume — videos from other users.

But beyond that, notifications use people's lives to attract others to spend time, without our really wanting it.

REINVENTION OF CORRESPONDENCE OR REIFICATION OF CONVERSATION CARRIERS?

What was until recently a reinvention of correspondence between individuals has taken a completely different path: a desire to merge, fuse, or conflict lives alongside or with others.

This desire is polymorphic, sometimes even contradictory.

A business desire on one side: in the most cynical approach, creating a dependency in a large mass of users, analyzable in real-time, who voluntarily return to spend their time and lives on a platform opens Pandora's box from a marketing perspective to sell products or ideas. In a more noble way, large-scale projects wanted critical masses to make an idea, a dream, possible: the SETI @ Home project was one of the first large-scale scientific experiments where users downloaded a tool to analyze signals from space in the hope of helping find extraterrestrial life; an old dream of humanity made alive through SETI[45]. Scientific examples are numerous, especially in cancer research where doctors, patients, hospital staff gather to share knowledge and co-create solutions.

CONTRADICTORY DESIRES

A desire from people themselves: the pleasure of meeting, romantically or not, around a common interest has allowed some to awaken a most pleasant, most gratifying side of their humanity.

A political desire as well, which for some is akin to Pascal's wager: connecting people would ultimately bring improvement.

Liveness is torn by different desires, different forces that clash through notifications. We have only limited attention for an exponentially growing desire for digital liveness; the risk is a problem of throughput with, at this stage, notifications occupying the user in a poorly prioritized manner — except for expert users who know how to configure their devices — which risks overvaluing certain applications rather than certain communities. By default, when someone buys a smartphone, apps are pre-installed; in most cases, this doesn't seem to pose a problem.

---

[45] https://setiathome.berkeley.edu/sah_papers/cacm.php

However, affirming the dominance of certain platforms even before turning on a smartphone is not neutral. It imposes that certain apps have more digital liveness.

"Franck said: money is the art of people (...) Someone who earns 1000 times more than their peers isn't necessarily someone who works 1000 times more or 1000 times better. It is someone whose art is to value the art of people".[46] Jacques Auberger

---

[46] https://www.youtube.com/watch?v=77U5ZcreS6o

AVATARIZATION OF LIVENESS?

As we have seen, digital liveness has taken shape due to technological revolutions that have introduced new social behaviors. Conversely, the actions of individuals themselves, whether intentional or accidental, can instigate new technological propositions: each time a user "hacks" (or modifies) a usage or functionality, the platform can decide to disseminate this functionality to all users. For example, when Instagram realized that users were taking screenshots of their favorite posts, it added the "save" feature, allowing the creation of inspiration boards. Liveness intensely listens to its members.

By becoming so integrated into our cultures and life habits, digital liveness has become almost a reflex. We first created fictions of ourselves — or at least accelerated the phenomenon — and the acceleration of technical and technological infrastructures can lead to a new stage of this fictionalization, close to a form of interfacing humans composed of new digital and physical properties.

VIRTUALIZATION OF FIGURES AND INSPIRATIONS: NEW FRONTIERS OF LIVENESS

Virtual influencers may have seemed anecdotal at their origins. When one of the first virtual influencers, Noonoouri, was created, many voices claimed the phenomenon would not catch on[47]. It is true, Noonoouri does not replace humans: she amplifies and extends individual identities by satisfying new needs. Her founder, Joerg Zuber, summarized the complementarity: "I think there is a positive coexistence between humans and digital

---

[47] https://www.vogue.com.au/vogue-codes/news/meet-noonoouri-the-virtual-instagram-influencer-loved-by-kim-kardashian-west-and-dior/news-story/dfeb2658e3bbc7b2cfd11d0d26eb5bbc

characters (…) [Noonoouri] needs human beings. She doesn't have a voice yet; she is an inch and a half tall. I took all these parameters into account so that she is clearly dependent on humans; she is always more powerful with a human than alone." In Japan, the number of (non-official) marriages between men and fictional characters has been accelerating since 2010. The term "moe" in Japanese describes the phenomenon where feelings can arise from a fictional being, akin to how nature blooms in life. A dreamlike but also technological vision, with the development of characters based on "super normal stimulus[48]," whose lucrative business further accelerates usage.

REAL, ARTIFICIAL: A SOCIETAL CHOICE

Honda Toru argues that "one day, soon, the hierarchy between real and artificial will no longer work (…) one day, we will accept that the world of dreams is a 'good' world, with warmth and comfort that cannot be found in human society[49]." Without wanting to fall into provocation, this maximalist vision of digital liveness worries me: schools, roads, hospitals, in short, a whole series of fundamental needs cannot be avatarized. I believe this analysis does not hold because the real issue is the intensity of digital liveness, the type of interfacing we will accept, and the underlying objective.

No child should believe that the warmth of a screen is more comforting than that of their parents. Nevertheless, the real/digital interfacing is indeed being deployed. Niantic announced in September 2022 the launch of "Lightship VPS," a new browser-based technology that

---

[48] https://bigthink.com/health/sexual-cartoons-are-supernormal-stimuli/
[49] https://www.theguardian.com/technology/2018/sep/26/mystic-messenger-dating-simulations-sims-digital-intimacy

anchors WebAR content to specific locations and allows virtual objects to interact with this space. "The introduction of Lightship VPS on the Web is a crucial advance for augmented reality, enabling developers to realistically merge digital content with the real world with precision and persistence."

In other words, every point on a world map can have a sort of digital anchor, generating an augmented reality experience. Niantic's goal is not to lead users to an external virtual world but to intensify the digital liveness of a very real physical location. Brain-Computer Interfaces (BCI) will also contribute to this merge of real surfaces or dimensions and perceived experience. Reinforcing even more digital liveness.

AND DEATH IN THIS LIVENESS?

The problem with digital liveness is undoubtedly that it has forgotten its own death.

Liveness relies on users who interact in more or less decentralized, more or less interconnected bubbles. Several cases of this death of digital liveness seem to be emerging.

WHEN USERS THEMSELVES DIE

A morbid vision of social networks, platforms' main engine is humans themselves. When they die, a considerable part of the network's value also disappears. Meta, likely due to its history, has worked on memorial pages, true online sanctuaries for the deceased. TikTok is also working on the subject, while users, as always ahead of usage, try to use existing features like slideshows to celebrate the dead. What is interesting is the return of the human in these cases: it is through memories, archives, stories of people around people, that this digital liveness is recreated, the digital bubble becoming merely an expression since the deceased can hardly respond.

WHEN PLATFORMS DIE

The internet, the web whether 2.0 or 3.0, is not made of flesh and bones but servers, cables, pipes, electronic components. Liveness to date has been carried by users on platforms created by private companies. These companies die and can take with them the billions of interactions, accounts, histories — and therefore the historicity — of their users. How many forums from the 90s - 2000s are still active today? A real issue for societies whose scope we still poorly measure.

WHEN USERS MIGRATE

Liveness, especially due to bubble phenomena, can wither when users migrate from one platform to another, or when a new generation of users decides to adopt another platform. Recent history has shown shifts from Facebook to Instagram, then to Snapchat or TikTok in France. Accounts can continue to be active, but their intensity decreases, leading to a loss of digital liveness.

Perhaps only ecosystems of meta-applications like WeChat or to a lesser extent Line can force users to keep their digital liveness in the same environment, the same giant bubble. Simply because the user has no choice.

PERSPECTIVES

We have created a living substance, digital liveness, born from our increasing interactions on social networks, platforms, or other metaverses. From this intensification of our connected existences, digital liveness has taken shape beyond our screens, a substance we feel, hope for, sometimes reject. Three little dots that have changed our humanity. Three little dots that invite us to consider the consequences of digital liveness.

THE SOCIAL BODY, THE PHYSICAL BODY, THE PRIVATIZED BODY

Liveness is neither good nor bad: it exists. The impacts on our social and physical lives open up several avenues for reflection.

Unlike other media we had to actively engage with, digital liveness is born and does not stop at will. It exists through us and affects us, positioning us. To date, it is controlled by private companies: they handle the infrastructure costs, develop the engineering around it, invest, recruit, and engage users. When the digital liveness emanating from certain platforms becomes massive, it quickly impacts the social body as a whole. Facebook has been repeatedly accused of promoting conspiracy theories, Instagram of encouraging anorexia among young people, and TikTok of inciting dangerous behaviors among young children. Often, it is only afterward that legislators or public authorities try, more or less effectively, to implement tools to protect users. A vast task when we know that opening Snapchat now makes it as easy to buy drugs as ordering a pizza on Deliveroo. French author & influencer Emery Doligé, summarizes: "The viewer or spectator wanted to forget their body to be overwhelmed by content."

The body in digital liveness and its billions of data points are orchestrated by businesses whose system still often relies on the time spent on their network, on their property. In other words, we give part of our lives to businesses that inherently have no real moral responsibility toward us. This raises an issue regarding the transmission of our digital livenesss to our children, which neither public authorities nor the platforms themselves have addressed; even for well-supported celebrities or artists, controversies emerge daily.

This digital liveness goes far beyond the scope of digital vaults, the solutions that banks, insurance companies, or even notaries are beginning to offer their clients. In its most extreme interpretations, digital liveness could be downloaded, creating a kind of double consciousness, onto computers, giving a semblance of immortality to billionaires. Once again, we see: digital liveness is a power issue; it desperately needs life so that digital liveness does not become a digital garden populated by spiritless entities.

A gigantic task proves that interfacing is already happening; just look at the average age at which a child starts using a touchscreen tablet to understand how much digital liveness will permeate the lives of all future generations.

STANDARDIZATION, LIVENESS CAPITAL, AND INDIVIDUALISM

Platforms may claim they aim to authentically reveal individuals' talents, but some strings of success remain the same.

In the pre-internet world, the principle for a store was "no parking, no business," meaning if customers couldn't park in front, there could be no sales. In the world of digital liveness, the number of "followers" or the score are still too often the two criteria for evaluating individuals. No followers, no digital liveness, one might say. This poses a significant problem of differentiation: if to exist, one must play by the platform's rules, and to be disseminated, one must meet a critical mass on it, what happens to the billions of possible talents who cannot express themselves on these platforms?

Conversely, TikTok has opened the floodgates compared to other networks like Instagram by allowing an exponential number of accounts to be followed by millions of people. Paradoxically, this approach has a problem: that millions of accounts are followed by millions of people. By creating this abundance of accounts - and followers to these accounts — there is a tipping point where creators may no longer have content worth an interesting price — since they compete with the millions of other followed accounts, like everyone else — while the number of followers will not necessarily mean interesting monetization or valorization for these accounts. TikTok sets the prices under the guise of democratization.

TikTok has anticipated the criticisms well by being one of the first actors to pay — modestly — content creators. A way to give a token to defuse value loss and control prices on its platform.

The question of censorship also arises: platforms are caught between a need to make cash — thus casting a wide net — even if it means accepting extremists, conspiracy theorists, in summary, an exacerbated range of the world's vices. Conversely, the "virtue" of platforms can seem very limited: censoring photos with women's nipples on Instagram under the guise of nudity prohibition, while the platform has consistently promoted and encouraged the publication of highly suggestive content, with Instagram's private messages being a hotspot for nudes (nude photos of users, temporarily visible — or not).

It's a paradox: digital liveness under technological amphetamines has weak, ineffective governance. It has become a force that impacts absolutely every aspect of society: education, security, social mobility; yet, platforms absolve themselves by placing the responsibility on users. An untenable stance in the long term: once "hooked," people would be left alone facing digital liveness, with the resulting inequalities, tensions, and violence. A new state of nature of each against each if governance is deserted. This is often the platforms' argument: not being able to moderate the most problematic content or users due to lack...of resources. And leaving it to the private actor (you, me) to handle the responsibility of usage, after doing everything to make the network a popular success. But certainly not a success with a collective mission.

Liveness becomes one of the most important capitals in the coming years: some individuals would be more in digital liveness than others on networks, platforms, or metaverses. And it is not just about entertainment but a capital that impacts every aspect of society, every function.

There is likely a role for public authorities to play in implementing "free" strategies to promote other forms of digital liveness. Or, less naively, an urgent need to compel platforms to adopt much stronger governance modes to make their systems more favorable to people.

The risk is to create new bubbles of rebellion, very effective for their own objectives, but with the flaws of cartels. This is already the case in the world of culture, where some collectives or crews share high-value information privately, set the value of an artist, a work, an idea, independently of its digital footprint alone.

It remains to be seen how other areas — particularly health or even politics — could propose their own models of digital liveness, independently of platforms, rather than following the trend and thus being subservient to them, without falling into exclusion or club logics.

Various actors propose some avenues:

- The creation of open-source social networks to give groups the ability to create their own mini platforms. Unfortunately, few examples have broken through at this stage, as providing the tool does not mean providing the plan or ingredients to build a society on these networks. The network Diaspora* had met with some success but never managed to reach critical mass.

- The governance of the platforms themselves could be subjected to much stricter rules; as we have seen, digital liveness is far from being just a technological issue but a societal one; before granting access to a network, perhaps we should imagine structures that could authorize the marketing of these applications; after all, in a quasi-dictatorial way, this is already the case in China. Therefore, a more democratic solution could be imagined between app stores (from Apple or Google) and public authorities. The argument that such control would kill innovation is weak: Apple already imposes very stringent constraints on developers; and the dream of French EdTech startups (an acronym for education technologies) is precisely to redefine relationships with the Ministry of Education.

- The European Union is equipping itself with a corpus of texts and rules to compel platforms: the excuse of only being subject to Californian law will probably not be viable in the long run.

- The promises of Web3 hint at certain possibilities via more decentralized systems to create networks where trust can be distributed.

ASSISTED MEMORIES, RECORDED HISTORY, REAL HISTORY

As mentioned, platforms die. All of them. In the era of recorded history, digital liveness is probably one of the future battles for historians of the next century. Because not everything is archived, saved forever: only the elements that platforms choose to preserve are; and a battle between suggested history — the memories pushed by platforms to users among the billions of possible contents — and real history is already underway.

The consecration of a viral phenomenon comes through a reprise in so-called traditional media, which will give a name to the phenomenon, give it a beginning and an end. The role of professional media is underestimated: over the last 20 to 30 years, the archiving effort of media like the New York Times remains more effective than looking for an old post on Facebook, not to mention Snapchat.

The archiving of digital liveness, its very historicity, raises the question of who is responsible: on Wikipedia, 80% of contributors are men, with underrepresented minorities, which worries about the analysis of the current world by future scientists[50].

When a business dies, what happens to the millions of messages generated? The exercise is striking when we search for old contributions or messages: between services that have gone bankrupt, platforms that have decided to restructure all their content entirely, systems that get bought out, few areas can ensure keeping our traces of digital liveness.

Proponents of post-truth have well understood the issue: one of the first tasks is to save videos — especially from opponents — and undertake an immense effort to remount

---

[50] https://www.nytimes.com/2016/06/26/magazine/how-an-archive-of-the-internet-could-change-history.html

sequences, to then disseminate these altered montages on social networks years later. And to use digital liveness to disseminate their worldview. Groups with a goal can define the tools to achieve their ends; ordinary users or actors on a platform without the same intensity in their objectives may see their truth disappear under this industrialization of archiving for manipulation purposes. Media education is essential, and especially education to digital liveness.

ALGORITHMIC SOCIALIZATION?

Another issue of this digital liveness is the socialization process itself; platforms involve very high user engagement to "exist more." But for a vast majority of users, their passive or casual consumption can lead to a more passive socialization, dependent on what platforms will submit to them. Isn't TikTok's For Your Page one of the most cynical principles, as if the individual were no longer able to make their choices and accept to get lost, to find gems?

Boredom seems to have turned into an enemy for platforms; an injunction to emit a signal of life even when the individual no longer wants to.

Solid institutions had already liquefied since Zygmunt Bauman's analyses, pushing frameworks like family, various churches, nations, into a state of major uncertainty, where the best-equipped to navigate are setting up new strategies of domination. Social networks — and this digital liveness in its most consumerist aspect — have forced a devaluation of certain sacred aspects. The faithful seem to be transforming into little gods, as if the sacred itself had melted into a very consumerist relationship.

The cases of Kanye West or Donald Trump are illuminating: have we created clickbait people after creating content designed to deceive people's attention[51]? "Just as the media had to create versions of clickbait, will we have to create our own versions of unhealthy personas?"

A socialization that thus rests on toxic fictions, pleasing because they allow for easy positioning for or against, to express viewpoints…and thus to exist oneself.

AGAINST ALGORITHMIC LIVENESS, THE REVENGE OF LANGUAGE

All is not set in stone with digital liveness; and while platforms, metaverses, networks try to frame it, humans' ability to trick what alienates them is underway.

The case of emojis and stickers on social networks is a notable case of rebellion.

Krish Raghav, artist and comic book illustrator, takes the example of WeChat and how Chinese users have developed indirect communication strategies to free themselves from platform control[52]. "Stickers become a means to create communities and dissonant expressions. (…) Perhaps stickers offer a hope that undisciplined improvisations can spring forth, no matter what digital platforms push us to believe is the new normal."

In other words, digital liveness finds its richness not in the explicit but in all the implicit mechanics that users create, operate, and recombine. It is this implicit that brings it to life in people's existence.

TikToks whisper cultural references to people, are shared on an instant messaging group with the family. A tweet is taken as proof in a family debate. A screenshot from Spotify is shared in an Instagram Story to evoke a

---

[51] https://nymag.com/intelligencer/2018/10/kanye-west-and-donald-trump-and-the-rise-of-human-clickbait.html

[52] https://tinyletter.com/reallifemag/letters/the-infinite-sadness

feeling, an emotion. The three little dots of a message being written captivate a lover, waiting for the promised response.

A series of emojis evokes a memory only two people can understand. An old photo of a friend gone too soon revives the pain of a group on Facebook. A grandfather missed a message on Telegram and gets thoroughly reprimanded by his sons. On Twitch, a commentator entertains thousands of football fans by commenting on a match 5000 kms from his bedroom. Someone has insomnia and wanders on forums, or seeks a bit of excitement on OnlyFans. It starts snowing, and a thousand Snaps on Snapchat talk about the weather. Far away, a witch streams her secrets live from Wisconsin on YouTube, before subscribers with thumbs up.

A world of relentless notifications, blurring benchmarks, pushing to focus on oneself, the world at the center of a hand holding a smartphone, insistently asking to reveal itself and to reveal the billions of connected people.

A hyper-reality that reminds us that in the end, what makes digital liveness, what gives it its strength, is the fact that it is humans who decide to give it life, by attributing a quasi-divine character to the distant. In three little dots.

ACKNOWLEDGMENTS

The family. The extended family. The Internet family.
Thomas Bucaille for his support.
Quentin Molina for everything.
Dreamers, critics, people who doubt, creatives.

It's good to be alive.

Follow me:

@lilzeon

aliveinsocialmedia.substack.com

o   o
—

...

2024

www.ingramcontent.com/pod-product-compliance
Lightning Source LLC
La Vergne TN
LVHW051536050326
832903LV00033B/4282